GRUMPY CAT

GRUMPY CAT

A GRUMPY BOOK

BY GRUMPY CAT

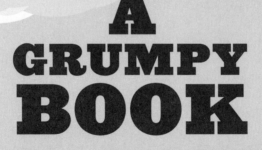

CHRONICLE BOOKS
SAN FRANCISCO

ISBN: 978-1-4521-2657-9

MIX
Paper from responsible sources
FSC® C016245
FSC
www.fsc.org

Manufactured in Canada
Designed by Kelly Abeln and Michael Morris

10 9 8 7 6 5 4

Chronicle Books LLC
680 Second Street
San Francisco, California 94107
www.chroniclebooks.com

Grumpy Cat

would like to thank . . .

~~Bryan Bundesen~~

~~Tabatha Bundesen~~

~~Ben Lashes~~

~~Kia Kamran~~

~~Emilie Sandoz~~

~~Kelly Abeln~~

~~Pokey~~

~~"Dog"~~

~~Cactus~~

NO ONE.

A Grumpy Introduction

I get a lot of questions about how I got to be as grumpy as I am. I give everyone the same answer: you have until the count of three to leave, or the claws come out.

You see, true grumpiness comes from inside–you have to feel it down to your core. Even if you weren't born with it like me, however, you can still develop a grumpy mindset. This book will help you achieve that.

Why help you? Here's why: I dream of a world in which everyone sulks in their own corner, occasionally emerging to judge one another and feel disgust for everything around them.

Within these pages, you'll find tips on how to be grumpy, a tour of my life (for inspiration), and activities, games, and more to get you in a bad mood.

Hopefully, you'll finally leave me alone.

INSINCERELY,
GRUMPY CAT

IT'S NOT ME
IT'S YOU

Forecast for Your Life

NOW THAT YOU HAVE THIS BOOK, things are going to start looking down for you right away. Here's the forecast for the rest of your life. No matter what the weather is outside, this is what it will be in your heart.

EVERY NEW
BEGINNING
ENDS

Think Grumpy

HERE'S WHY *YOU* GET GRUMPY:

- I have to wake up too early.
- My foot hurts.
- What's that smell?
- It's raining.

HERE'S WHY *I* GET GRUMPY:

- I have to wake up.
- I have feet.
- The world has smells in it.
- Anything.

TRUE GRUMPINESS is about embracing the horrible in everything that happens every day.

REMEMBER: IT'S *ALL* BAD.

I HAD FUN ONCE
IT WAS AWFUL

I HATE
MORNING PEOPLE
AND MORNINGS
AND PEOPLE

Getting In a Grumpy Mood

Having some trouble sustaining your grumpiness?

Here are some negative facts and statistics to get you in the right space:

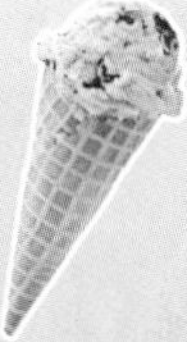

Eating yummy ice cream cones often results in permanent, incurable brain freezes.

Puppies like to trick people into starting wars. At least 65% of wars are caused by puppy trickery.

Flowers are cesspools of bee urine and hummingbird spit.

Cute, laughing babies are responsible for 99.5% of horrible diseases in the world.

In a beautiful park on a sunny day, the trees are full of squirrels waiting to drop rocks on your head.

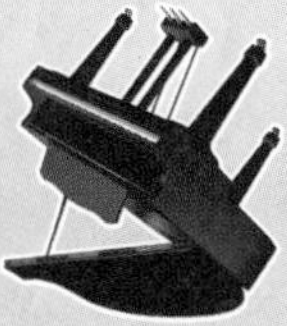

Happy people are two times more likely to get hit by falling pianos than unhappy people are.

A single kiss contains more germs than 100 toilet seats.

GRUMPY *Moments*

MY HOME

I live in Arizona. Ever heard of it? I don't care.

Arizona is mostly barren and devoid of life.

There's a lot of dirt and sticks.

It's not all desert. Sometimes there's something green, like a tree. Which is the worst.

Here's some grass. I'd like to bury you under it.

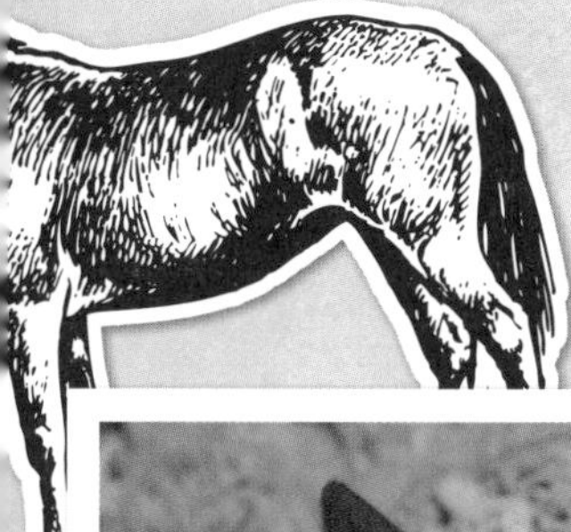

But a lot of the time Arizona is just rocks and sand and burning sun.

I avoid direct contact with the outdoors whenever possible.

TIME HEALS
ALL WOUNDS
I BROKE
YOUR WATCH

STOP AND SMELL
THE ROSES
I SAW SOME
ON THE FREEWAY

A Grumpy Past, Present, and Future

PAST

PRESENT

0

Born frowning.

3 MONTHS

My first word: No.
My second word: Good.

8 MONTHS

Had fun. It was awful.

1 YEAR

Become famous Internet cat. Destroy the hopes and dreams of millions. Good.

14 YEARS

Inspire new kind of plastic surgery that gives you a permanently frowny face.

35 YEARS

Invent dog incapable of barking, licking, or smiling. Make lots of money. Burn it.

48 YEARS
Become first cat president of the United States following groundbreaking "I don't care about this country or you" campaign. Don't do anything while in office. Run country into ground. Good.

70 YEARS
Unintentionally eliminate threat of global warming with cold, cold stare.

FUTURE

65 YEARS Reduce countless people and animals to tears.

100 YEARS
Become the only cat to live 100 years, having learned from old people that the less you enjoy life, the longer you will be forced to endure it. Continue to live probably forever.

GRUMPY *Moments*

MY ROOMMATES

Pokey is my biological brother. There's not much of a resemblance.

This dog is horrible. Frankly, I don't even know his name.

This is Cactus.
He's just a cactus with googly eyes. He's ok, I guess.

Here are the arms that belong to the humans we live with. They're always scooping me up. This was probably my worst day.

Nope, this was.

YOU ONLY
LIVE ONCE
ONE TIME
TOO MANY

Why I Hate... Dogs

HAPPY, CURIOUS, LOYAL...UGH.
LIKE TO SNIFF INAPPROPRIATE PLACES. WITH A WET, COLD NOSE.
ALWAYS LICKING, BARKING, PANTING.
COME EQUIPPED WITH FURRY WHIPS.
SMELLS LIKE A WET DOG.

How to Be Grumpy

Being grumpy is an art. It comes naturally for some of us (me). But for most it takes a lifetime of practice. But with a few simple tips, anyone can get started on the road to grumpiness at any age.

Here are a few tricks to try:

SITUATION	RESPONSE
Someone makes a joke or seems to be looking for approval.	Shake your head in embarrassment for them. Refuse to meet their eyes, exhale loudly, and rub your forehead. Repeat as necessary until they leave the room in discomfort.
You come up against a problem.	Don't ask for a helping hand. Try to remember that whatever you're working on isn't important anyway. Just don't do it.
You have a spare moment.	Look around you and try to think of at least one judgmental thing to say about something. The goal is to see nothing but disappointment and failure.
You find yourself feeling hopeful or optimistic.	Dig down and remember that you are an insignificant speck on this planet and your life is meaningless.

IF YOU DON'T
HAVE ANYTHING
NICE TO SAY
GOOD

Anatomy of a Frown

1. Eyes simultaneously judge you and think you are too boring to care
2. Eyeballs bug out a bit in disbelief and disgust
3. Brow furrows just slightly
4. Chin out, but not so much that you look proud or something
5. Edges of mouth approach chin
6. Top of mouth approaches nose
7. Ears: feel free to experiment and find what works best for you

Even if you're not yet completely grumpy, you can help yourself get there by *looking* grumpy.

CULTIVATE YOUR FROWN AND THE REST WILL FOLLOW.

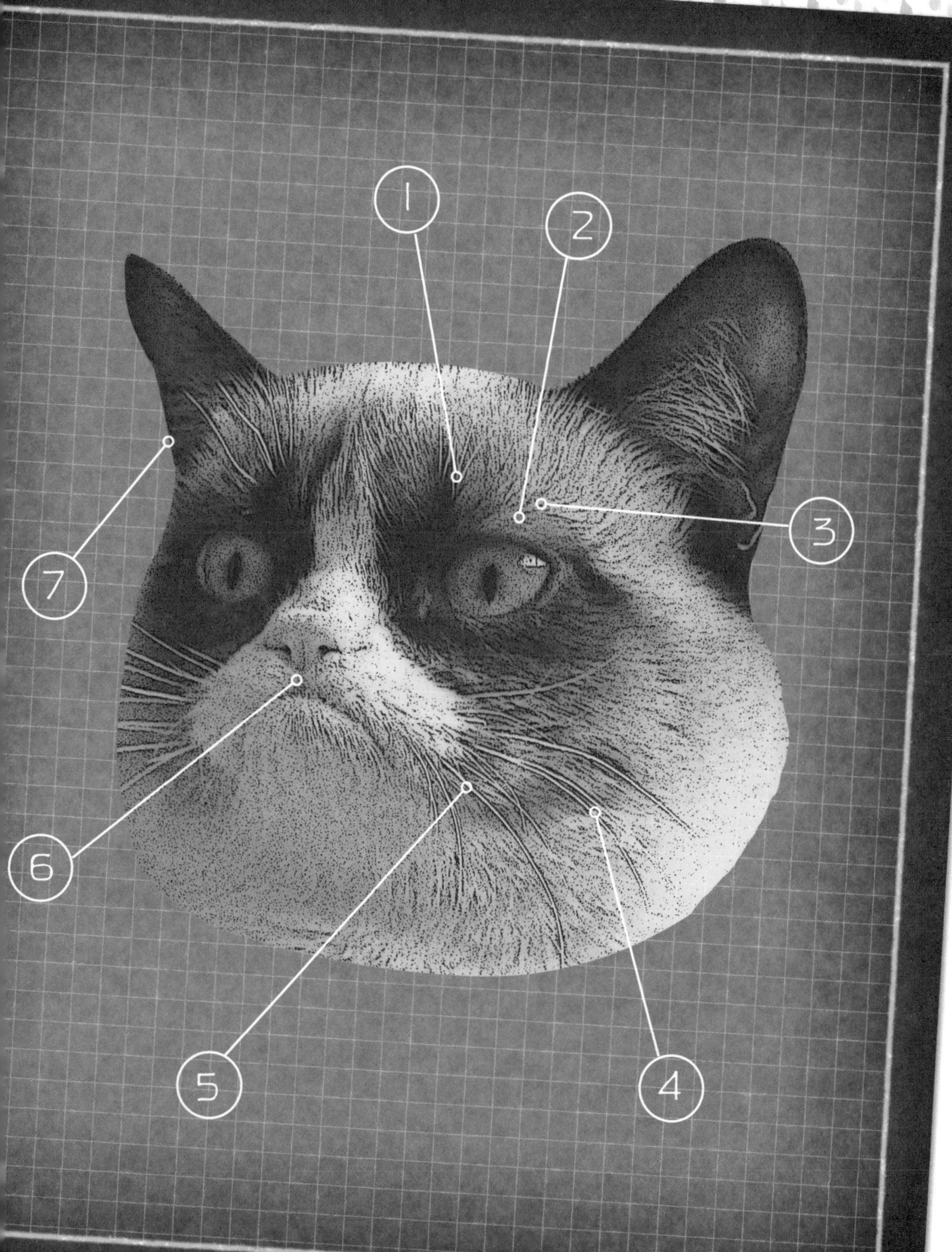

1
2
3
4
5
6
7

GRUMPY *Moments*

MY LIFE

I usually celebrate my birthday by blowing out someone else's candles before they have a chance.

I tried to teach Pokey to be grumpy. It didn't work.

Here's me and Cactus. We don't talk much, we mostly just stare off into space and think about things we dislike.

And other things.

Oh, dog. He constantly tortures me with kisses.

IF YOU'RE HAPPY
AND YOU KNOW IT
GET AWAY
FROM ME

From the Desk of Grumpy Cat

TO DO TODAY

- [x] JUDGE YOU
- [x] JUDGE YOUR FACE
- [x] EAT BREAKFAST
- [x] EAT YOUR BREAKFAST
- [x] MAKE LITTLE BOY CRY
- [ ] MAKE OLD LADY CRY
- [ ] HANG OUT WITH CACTUS
- [x] MAKE FUN OF DOG
- [ ] GO TO SLEEP AND WAIT FOR ANOTHER TERRIBLE DAY

Frown File

If you master each of the following looks, you can effectively ruin anyone's day.

LOOK

MEANING

Stare = Sullen

Leer = Angry

Glower = Gloomy

Glare = Disgusted

Look in a mirror and practice until you're not terrible.

Pop Quiz!

MATCH THE EXPRESSION TO THE SITUATION.

Now that you're a frown expert, prove it. Match the grumpy expression to the happy occasion in order to ruin it for everyone.

A

B

C

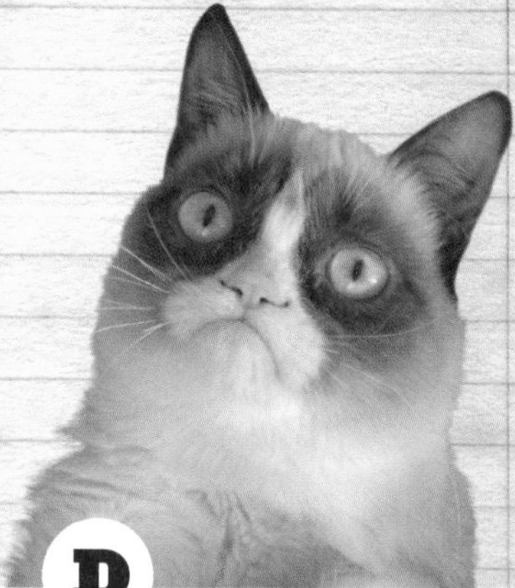

D

1

2

3

4

ANSWERS: 1, C; 2, A; 3, B; 4, D

Grumpy Word Hunt

JUST HOW GRUMPY ARE YOU?

See how many times you can find the word "grumpy" in the puzzle below.

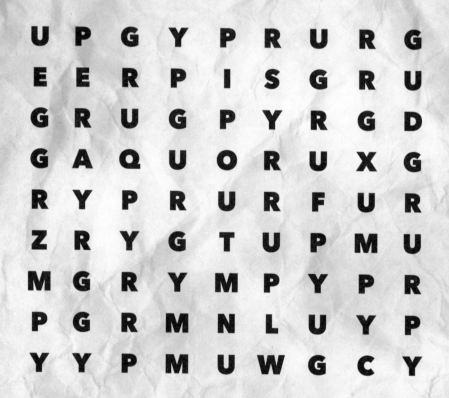

U	P	G	Y	P	R	U	R	G
E	E	R	P	I	S	G	R	U
G	R	U	G	P	Y	R	G	D
G	A	Q	U	O	R	U	X	G
R	Y	P	R	U	R	F	U	R
Z	R	Y	G	T	U	P	M	U
M	G	R	Y	M	P	Y	P	R
P	G	R	M	N	L	U	Y	P
Y	Y	P	M	U	W	G	C	Y

ANSWER: You fail. No, it doesn't matter why.

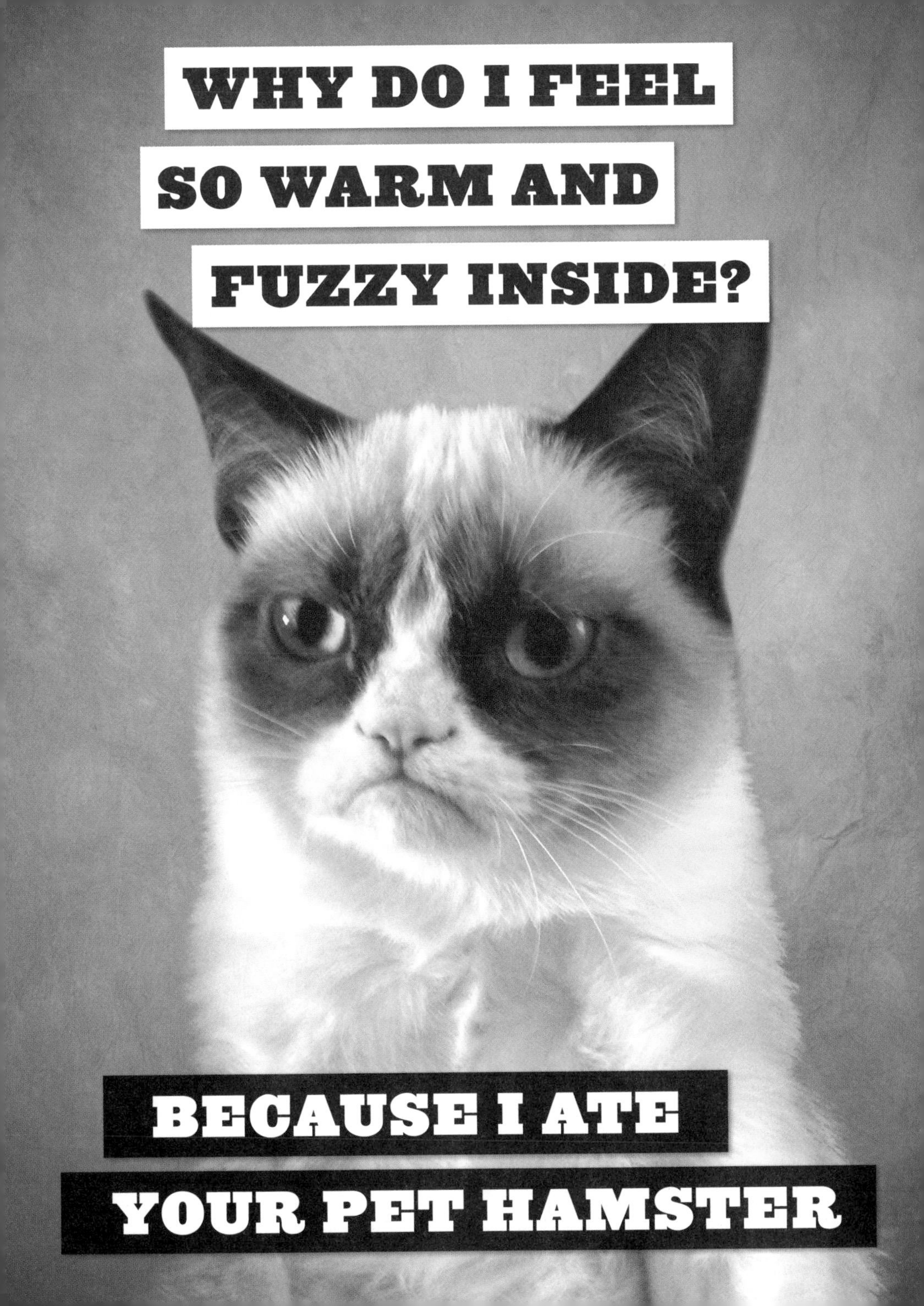
WHY DO I FEEL
SO WARM AND
FUZZY INSIDE?
BECAUSE I ATE
YOUR PET HAMSTER

LIFE IS LIKE A BOX
OF CHOCOLATES
BUT THOSE
AREN'T CHOCOLATES

Connect the dots to reveal my worst nightmare.

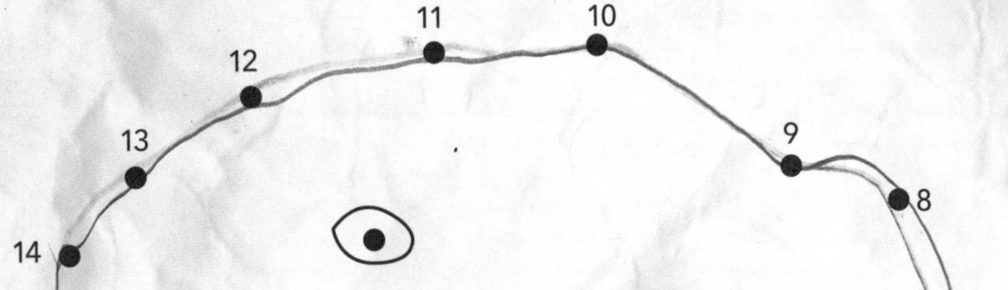

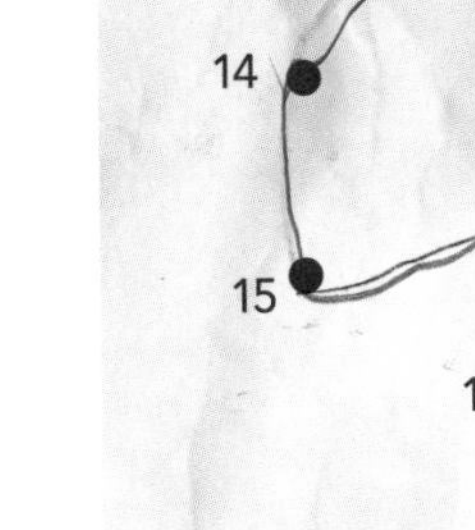

ANSWER: A dog that is happy and wants to cuddle.

Demotivational Posters

Sometimes even the grumpiest grumps need inspiration to stay grumpy.

LOVE IS . . .
TO BE AVOIDED AT ALL COSTS.

BE
MISERABLE!

A friend
is someone who doesn't know
how much you hate them.

Just give up.

Frown and the
world frowns
with you.

If you hate something,
set it free. If it returns
to you, destroy it.

VISUALIZE GRUMPINESS

If you're having trouble unleashing your inner grump, try this meditation exercise:

Close your eyes, take a deep breath, and envision the following . . .

You're walking barefoot through the forest. Sunlight filters through the trees. The moss is soft beneath your feet.

You step onto a log to get a better view . . .

. . . and you get a giant splinter wedged in between your toes.

A bluebird serenades you from a nearby branch, keeping time to the musical babble of the brook that flows through the forest . . .

. . . and it poops on you. When you look up, it poops again. In your eye.

You glimpse a shimmering unicorn through the foliage . . .

. . . and as it gets closer, you realize it's just a horse with an ice cream cone stuck to its head.

THERE ARE TWO
KINDS OF PEOPLE
IN THIS WORLD
I'D PREFER ZERO

GRUMPY Moments

TIMES I'VE BEEN ARRESTED

Disorderly conduct

Making a policeman cry

Making a dog cry

Ruining Christmas

Incorrectly using a sandbox

Grumpy in Translation

PARLEZ-VOUS GRUMPAIS? HABLAS GRUMPAÑOL? SPRECHEN SIE GRÜMPY?

It's easy to be grumpy around the world. If someone asks you a question, here's how to respond in several different languages.

VENEZIA
ENGLISH: NO
ITALIAN: NO
CHINESE: 没有
FRENCH: NON

I TRIED LOOKING
ON THE BRIGHTER
SIDE OF LIFE
IT HURT MY EYES

I HAVE AN IDEA
GO AWAY

What's making me Grumpy?

Draw something for me to judge.

ANSWER: You should have drawn a self-portrait. You are a constant disappointment to me.

From the Desk of Grumpy Cat

SHOPPING LIST

- [x] DOG REPELLENT
- [ ] PEOPLE REPELLENT
- [x] HAMSTER (TELL PET STORE YOU INTEND TO KEEP IT AS A PET. TRY NOT TO LAUGH MANIACALLY.)
- [ ] AFTERNOON SNACKS (MORE HAMSTERS?)
- [x] STUPID HAT TO FORCE ON OWNERS AND TAKE THEIR STUPID PICTURE

WHAT DOESN'T
KILL YOU
ISN'T WORKING

THEY SAY YOUR
FACE USES MORE
MUSCLES TO FROWN
THAN TO SMILE
I LIKE TO
STAY IN SHAPE

Why I Hate . . . Kittens

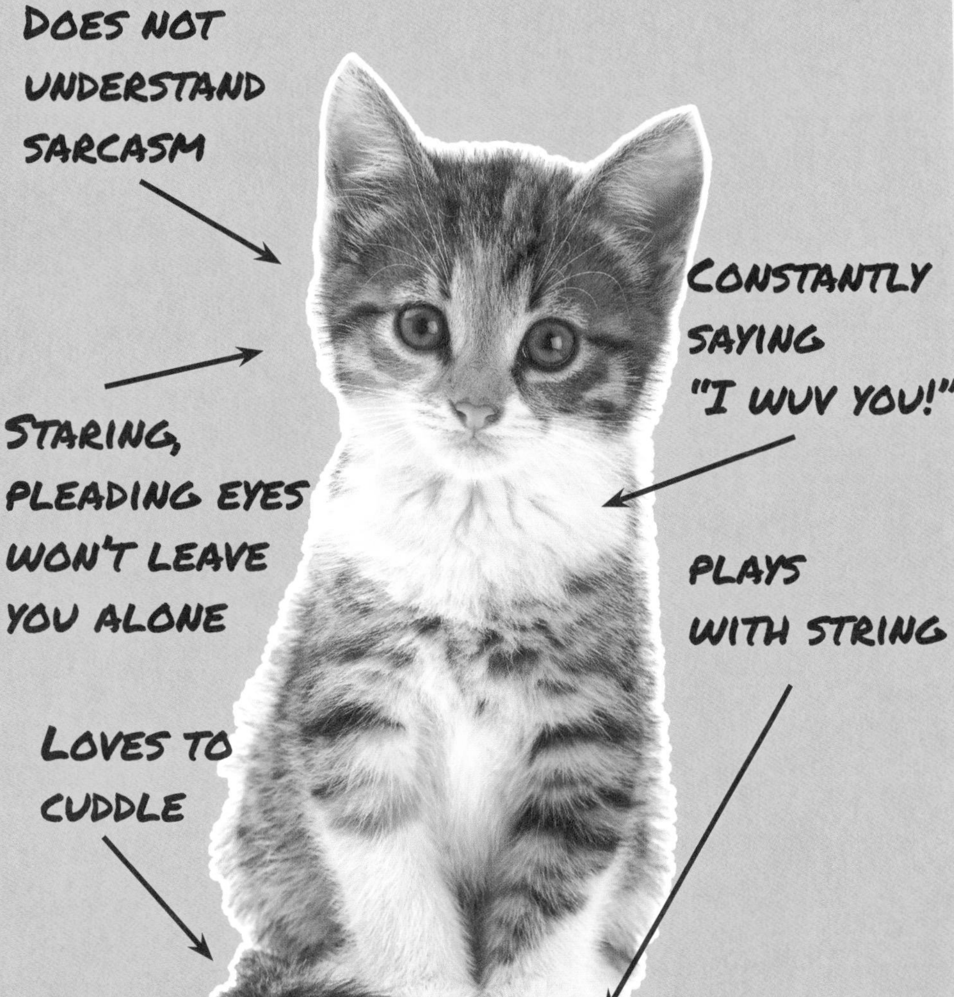

Grumpy Crossword Puzzle

ACROSS

1. The opposite of "yes"
2. "____ way, Jose"
3. A two-letter abbreviation for "number"
4. Aren't babies the cutest??
5. James Bond villain Dr. ____
6. Word used to signal a negative response
7. He pitched a ___-hitter (in baseball)
8. Jean-Paul Sartre play "____ Exit"
9. "____ means no"
10. Would you like fries with that?

DOWN

1. A two-letter abbreviation for "North"
2. U.S. education law, ____ Child Left Behind
3. Can you give me a hand here?
4. Symbol for the synthetic element Nobelium
5. Def Leppard song "No No ___"
6. A two-letter abbreviation for New Orleans
7. An anagram of "on"
8. "____ two ways about it"
9. Can we be friends?
10. Abbreviation for Nitric oxide

ANSWERS: Across (1. No 2. No 3. No 4. No 5. No 6. No 7. No 8. No 9. No 10. No) Down (1. No 2. No 3. No 4. No 5. No 6. No 7. No 8. No 9. No 10. No)

1 no
2 no
3 no
4 no
5 no
6 no
7 no
8 no
9 no
10 no
o

Grumpy Monuments

Since the beginning of time, humans have erected monuments to grumpiness. These great wonders of the world have long served to make happy people stop smiling and start frowning.

Help me Get to the Fun Ball of String!

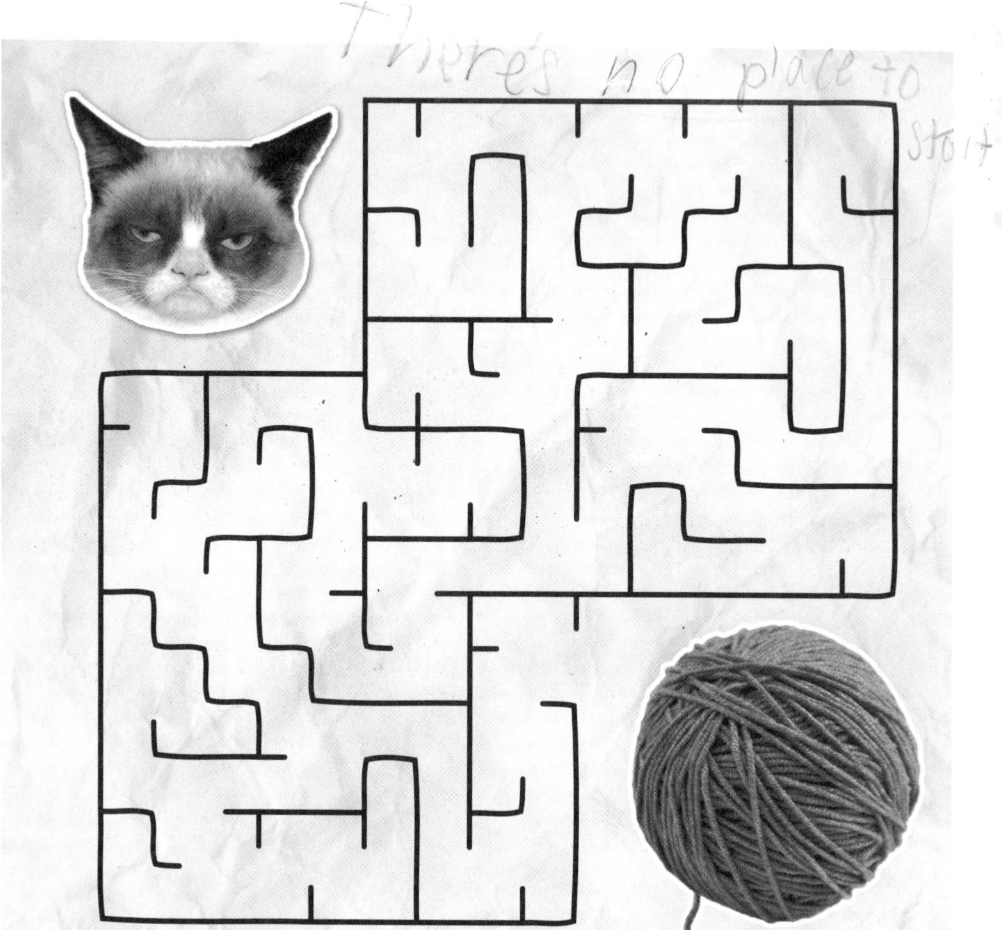
There's no place to start

ANSWER: That was a test. I locked all the doors to the maze and refuse to participate. You failed.

I'D HAVE THE
LAST LAUGH
BUT MY FACE DOESN'T
MAKE THAT SHAPE

GRUMPY *Moments*

HISTORICAL OCCASIONS I'VE RUINED

The moon landing

The signing of the Declaration of Independence

The voyage of the *Titanic*

The Shackleton Expedition

The fall of the Berlin Wall

Connect the dots to reveal how I'm feeling.

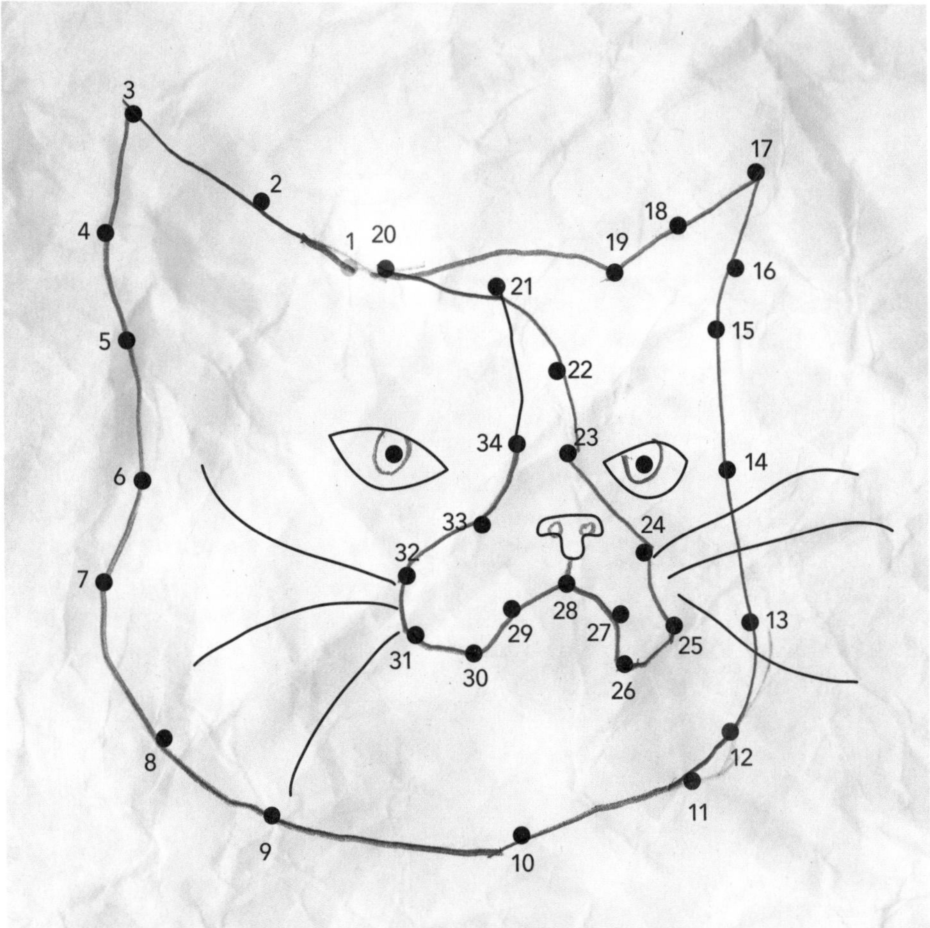

ANSWER: Was there really any question?

I LIKE MY HUMANS
THE WAY I LIKE
MY COFFEE
I HATE COFFEE

Grumpy Reading List

When you can't seem to shake that good mood, try one of these classic works of grumpy literature.

ROMEO & JULIET
IS A GREAT
LOVE STORY
THEY BOTH DIE

Grumpy Word Search

Find the uninspiring words in the puzzle below.

ABYSMAL	~~GRUMPY~~	~~NO~~	SPITEFUL	UNWELCOME
AWFUL	HORRIBLE	ODIOUS	~~TERRIBLE~~	WORTHLESS
DREADFUL	LOUSY	PESSIMIST	UNHAPPY	ZERO
FAIL	MEAN	~~QUIT~~	UNPLEASANT	

E	W	U	I	F	Z	E	S	U	P	O	I	I	S	S	F
P	A	J	N	L	J	O	O	H	S	I	D	C	A	Y	S
E	N	E	H	U	R	S	L	W	M	A	L	O	J	J	G
S	R	H	A	M	Q	I	N	G	R	U	M	P	Y	E	S
I	K	E	O	B	Q	U	I	T	F	A	I	L	C	M	Z
T	A	G	D	R	Y	D	T	E	R	R	I	B	L	E	E
Z	E	A	I	O	R	S	T	W	U	S	D	E	E	A	R
Y	K	A	O	I	A	I	M	D	N	A	S	S	M	N	O
H	Q	S	U	L	P	S	B	A	P	S	W	O	N	F	E
H	T	G	S	S	S	K	L	L	L	M	Q	O	E	T	F
N	J	E	R	O	F	U	N	W	E	L	C	O	M	E	E
T	O	E	E	N	F	D	R	E	A	D	F	U	L	C	Y
T	R	T	S	W	E	L	P	E	S	S	I	M	I	S	T
S	R	G	A	H	Y	U	N	H	A	P	P	Y	U	R	Z
I	P	E	D	S	X	L	N	Q	N	T	E	O	X	R	C
S	K	Z	E	M	C	W	O	R	T	H	L	E	S	S	G

ANSWER: I don't have time for this.

I'VE LIVED
NINE LIVES
AND THIS IS
THE WORST

GRUMPY *Moments*

OCCASIONS I'VE RUINED

This baby's birthday party

This baby shower

This old lady's birthday party

This presidential inauguration

This wedding

How to Host a Grumpy Party

Who knows why you're hosting a party. Maybe a dog is forcing you, or someone you hate has died and you want to celebrate. Whatever the reason, use the party as an opportunity to get everyone in a bad mood.

ATMOSPHERE:

- ☐ No music
- ☐ A clock that ticks loudly
- ☐ Hold party during thunderstorm if possible

DECORATIONS:

- ☐ One dozen (or more) black balloons
- ☐ Wilting flowers
- ☐ Something sticky spilled on the rug and slightly dried

FOOD:

LITTER BOX CAKE

Ingredients:

One chocolate cake from a mix

One white cake from a mix

One box instant vanilla pudding

One 16-ounce package white sandwich cookies

12 Tootsie Rolls

Special materials:

Plastic wrap

New, unused cat litter box

Litter scoop

Directions:

Prepare chocolate cake and white cake mixes and bake according to package instructions. Let cool, then crumble both cakes into a large bowl. Set aside. Prepare instant vanilla pudding according to the package instructions. Chill until set. Roughly crumble white sandwich cookies in a blender or in a plastic bag using a rolling pin. Mix half of the cookie crumbs and all of the cake crumbs with enough of the chilled pudding to get the mixture moist. Line a new cat litter box several times with plastic wrap so that the food doesn't touch the sides of the box. Scoop the cake crumb mixture into the box in an even layer. Unwrap 12 Tootsie Rolls. Heating them 2–3 at a time, warm them in the microwave for 20–30 seconds until pliable, then roll to create a realistic poo look. Scatter them on top of cake. Evenly distribute remaining cookie crumbs on top. Serve with litter scoop.

DRINK:

Add a few drops green and a few drops red food coloring to a gallon of milk. Serve at room temperature.

Grumpy Gift Guide

WHAT DO YOU GET THE PERSON WHO DOESN'T DESERVE ANYTHING?

Here are a few gift suggestions for when you're fresh out of ideas. They'll dampen the mood on any occasion, from the holidays to patriotic celebrations and beyond.

New scratching post

THERE'S NO "I"
IN TEAM
THERE'S NO
"YOU" EITHER

Motivational poster

Deluxe doorstop

Trip to an all-you-can-eat salad bar

Ergonomic litter box

Bouncing ball

I GOT YOU
A PRESENT
CHECK THE
LITTER BOX

I'LL BURN
THAT BRIDGE
WHEN I
COME TO IT

ABSENCE MAKES
THE HEART
GROW FONDER
OF YOUR ABSENCE

Connect the dots to see what I had to say when the neighbor's dog went to go "live on the farm."

THE ART OF GRUMPY CONVERSATION

EARLY TO BED,
EARLY TO RISE
MAKES ME WANT
TO CLAW OUT
YOUR EYES

ABCDE
FU

Grumpy Coloring Time

Give Grumpy Cat a new look!

Acceptable colors: gray, dark gray, black.

Escape the Dog

THIS DOG WANTS TO PLAY.

Little does the dog know that I am leading him into danger, having set up numerous booby traps along the way. Help me get through the maze, avoiding the traps and arriving home safely (and solo).

IT'S A DOG EAT
DOG WORLD
GOOD

In Case of Happiness

We've reached the end of the book, which means you've either learned how to be grumpy or you haven't. Either way, I think we should go our separate ways. Here are some parting tips:

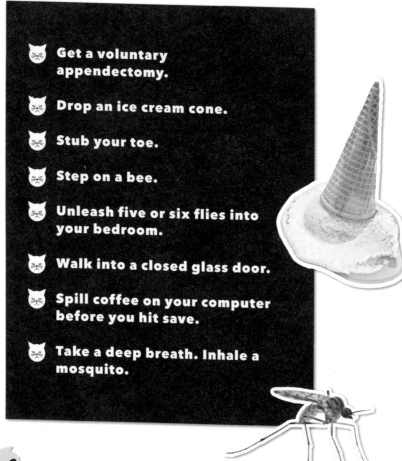

- **Get a voluntary appendectomy.**
- **Drop an ice cream cone.**
- **Stub your toe.**
- **Step on a bee.**
- **Unleash five or six flies into your bedroom.**
- **Walk into a closed glass door.**
- **Spill coffee on your computer before you hit save.**
- **Take a deep breath. Inhale a mosquito.**

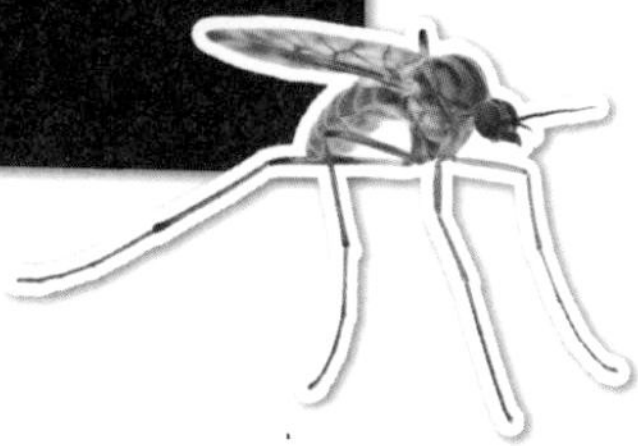

TURN THAT SMILE
UPSIDE DOWN

I WROTE A
BOOK ONCE
IT WAS AWFUL